Lindenhurst

Lindenhurst

✦

First Fifty Years

Joseph W. Brysiewicz

iUniverse, Inc.
New York Bloomington Shanghai

Lindenhurst
First Fifty Years

iUniverse books may be ordered through booksellers or by contacting:

iUniverse
1663 Liberty Drive
Bloomington, IN 47403
www.iuniverse.com
1-800-Authors (1-800-288-4677)

Because of the dynamic nature of the Internet, any Web addresses or links contained in this book may have changed since publication and may no longer be valid.

The views expressed in this work are solely those of the author and do not necessarily reflect the views of the publisher, and the publisher hereby disclaims any responsibility for them.

ISBN: 978-0-595-50704-7 (pbk)
ISBN: 978-0-595-61618-3 (ebk)

Printed in the United States of America

Contents

Acknowledgements

This book is the product of great dedication on the part of many people working together to bring the village of Lindenhurst a proper history, in honor of its Fiftieth Anniversary. If there is one over-arching principle I have learned about Lindenhurst through my research, it is this: ever since incorporation in 1956, the citizens of the village have demanded the very best of their government, their neighbors, and themselves. I can only hope this humble effort lives up to a strong tradition.

Thanks to those who helped drive this project and found the means to support it to fruition. Credit goes to the Village of Lindenhurst Board, First American Bank (Lindenhurst Branch), Friends of the Library (Lake Villa District Library), Lake County Board Chair Suzi Schmidt, and Mayor James Betustak—who first envisioned a history of Lindenhurst; he planted the seed. Further, I thank Jan Betustak, whose own research pointed me in many helpful directions when I came upon a dead end in writing this book. To Village Administrator James Stevens, who helped overcome practical obstacles in bringing this project to production, and for his many years of service to the village. These people and groups have created the book in your hands.

Thanks to all those who were dedicated to this project and the general belief that the preservation of local history must start in the present. Lake Villa Township is unusually blessed with those who have taken pains to preserve and write our history: Karen Loftus, Julie Trychta, Joyce Proper, Candace Saunders, Norbert Pischke, and Michael Polsgrove are among the few. I am indebted to their scholarship. In addition, much credit must be given to those who have donated their memories and photos to the Lindenhurst history archive—their material makes this project so rich. Of particular note is the dedication of former Village Clerk Judith A. Kempher whose dedication in seeking out and archiving the Village's past in the spring of 1981 forms the foundation of many pages herein. Thanks to the Lake Villa District Library, for allowing access to scanners, meeting rooms, and any other outrageous service I could dream up. Special credit goes to Kelly DiDonato for her belief in this project and to Lawrence Clayton whose dedication to this work was only eclipsed by his engaging conversation during my research. Certainly, the Lindenhurst History Committee has supported this vision from the start and has helped me in numerous ways—not least of which was temporarily moving the Village's historical archives to the Lake Villa District Library so I could research late into the night.

The Lindenhurst History Committee members are as follows:

Lisa Berg (Chair)
Joyce Dever (Co-Chair)
Kelly DiDonato
Richard Frank
Carol Larsen
Jim Streicher (a Lindenhurst institution in his own right)

A hearty thank you goes to Joyce Dever, who has done extensive research on Lindenhurst's earliest schools, and who is responsible for many images within this book, including the beautiful front-cover photograph. I should also mention here that Lisa Berg has truly balanced her busy life to help bring me onto this project. She has also obliged my demanding pleas and offered me whatever I needed. Thank you.

A brief note about sources: most material in this book can be found in either the Lake Villa District Library Historical Archives or the Lindenhurst Village Historical Archives. Photographs came from these two sources as well. Further, the Lake Forest College and Newberry Libraries helped me gain context and insight on the 19th century Sand Lake. My previous work on Lake Villa Township and metropolitan Chicago has helped me to find the narratives, particularly regarding Lindenhurst's role in the larger American story.

This is a very personal project for me. I spent the best years of my youth on Ironwood Drive, fishing and riding my bike in McDonald Woods, swimming in Lake Linden, and playing in Howard Bonner's cornfield—I believed it to be an extension of my back yard. Thanks to my parents, Gwen and Walter Brysiewicz, whose decision to move our family to the village has paid dividends, and to my brother Neil—a companion in those memories. To Christopher Puchli, my first friend and fellow explorer; we spent a childhood discovering the "true" Lindenhurst. Finally, thanks to my confidant, critic, editor and wife, Erin Lucido Brysiewicz. There has never been a limit to her support—something I have sorely tested during this process.

There are always others to thank; some overlooked, some forgotten. Their omission is my error and does not lessen their contributions. Let this be their acknowledgement. Here is a history in honor of Lindenhurst's first fifty years. Despite the best efforts of those named above, there are surely errors contained within; they are mine.

Joseph W. Brysiewicz
Spring, 2008

1

Before There Was Lindenhurst

The Land and the People

Any town's history is founded, quite literally, in the landscape it occupies. In the case of Lindenhurst, geography has defined and directed its development from a small farming community to an early example of that American phenomenon: the post-war commuter suburb.

Geographically, Lindenhurst is located fifty miles northwest of Chicago and just four miles south of the Illinois-Wisconsin state border. Originally part of McHenry County when Illinois became a state in 1818, Lindenhurst is now located in north central Lake County. The township system puts Lindenhurst in the eastern half of Lake Villa Township, which itself was created from the southern portion of Antioch Township, the northern portion of Avon Township, and small section of Grant Township in 1913.

Geologically, Northeastern Illinois is the product of a glacial retreat during the waning of the last Ice Age—approximately 13,000 and 14,000 years ago. This drawn-out process ended in excessive topological variation across the whole of the Northern United States, but in this area it carved out lakes and valleys in some places while depositing sediment and rock in others. The region lies within the Valparaiso moraine, a glacial sediment rise that rings Lake Michigan on its western and southern shores. Pockets of remaining ice created many of the lakes throughout the region, especially to the west in the Chain O' Lakes region.

Another gift of the glaciers is the soil of Lindenhurst itself, a particularly fertile loam, though according to a local history commemorating the Illinois' centennial history (1918), farmers needed to add "nitrogen and ground limestone for the most profitable agriculture." The region's earliest European settlement consisted of farms rather than residential streets. Nevertheless, the region's many uneven swamps, sloughs, and sinkholes proved a constant challenge for the wary landowner and settler.

1

It is fitting then that the first people of this region did not sustain themselves on intensive farming. The Potawatomi Indian who inhabited the area supplemented their agriculture with extensive fishing and hunting. When an early white expedition led by Colbee Benton came to the region in the 1830s, he documented the thriving Potawatomi population of the region in the *Journal to the Far-Off West*. Specifically, he referenced their frequent movement on a trail system that included a route from the Chain O' Lakes to Lake Michigan. Lindenhurst would have been part of this journey.

Benton unknowingly recorded the end of a prosperous way of life for all of the region's native populations. By 1830, the pressure of westward expansion by white settlers had reached the doorstep of Northeastern Illinois. A series of treaties—including a major land transfer brokered by a Chicago-led council in the autumn of 1833—involving the Potawatomi, the Sauk, and the Blackhawk ended Indian dominance of their land. By 1835, all but a few Potawatomi had relocated, by choice or by force, to west of the Mississippi. White settlement would now begin in earnest.

Most of the earliest settlers were Americans from the east coast, drawn to the inexpensive land and relative lack of Indian presence. The earliest recorded white settler to the Lake Villa township region was Pennsylvanian Noer Potter and his son Tingley in 1837. Their farm lay at the intersection of Monaville Road and Milwaukee Avenue (Route 83). They were quickly followed by the Christopher Manzer family and others. These initial settlers faced harsh conditions and relative isolation from both Chicago and even the nearer settlements of Little Fort (Waukegan) and Independence Grove (Libertyville).

William Bonner (Lindenhurst Village Archives)

Not all of the region's settlers were American. One unique facet that Lindenhurst and Lake Villa shared was the preponderance of English, German, and Scottish arrivals. In particular, families such as the Huckers and Barnstables came from Somerset, England, while the now disestablished post office of Monaville (west of Lindenhurst, south of Lake Villa) was named for the number of settlers hailing from the Isle of Man. Among the first white settlers to the Lindenhurst region were William Bonner and his family, émigrés from Aberdeenshire, Scotland. By 1842, the Bonner family had established Bonnie Brae, one of the earliest working farms in the area. Robert Strang would not create the nearby settlement of Millburn for another six years. Interestingly, the original Bonner farmstead only stopped operation in the early 1990s, when Howard "Shorty" Bonner sold the farm to developers; it became the residential subdivision known as Country Place.

The Post Offices: Sand Lake and Millburn

The post offices came first. Often little more than a collection of homes with a dry goods store or two, these pre-cursors to our modern towns were the center of settlements throughout Lake County. As 19th century settlers claimed the land in and around the Lindenhurst area, people required basic services and a way to organize themselves in a community. The farmer, however, had little time in his schedule to run extensive local governments. The earliest area post offices were Monaville and Angola, to the west of present-day Lindenhurst. By 1848, the Millburn Post Office was established (although it was sometimes referred to as Strang's Neighborhood).

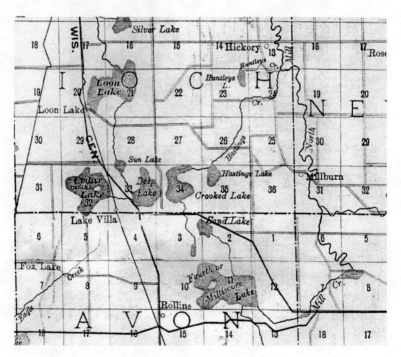

An early map showing the Sand Lake and Millburn Post Offices
(Lake Forest College Library)

Millburn offers a particularly excellent example of what a pioneer post office looked like. Also a well-known stop on the Underground Railroad for fugitive slaves, Millburn is one of the best-preserved 19th century settlements in Illinois, if not all of the Midwest. The Bonner family received their post here, along with many other Scottish families in the area. The name Millburn itself is Scottish for Mill Creek. Centered on the broken intersection between Route 45, Grass Lake Road, and Millburn Road, one can still feel the sense of the small settlement, the close community, and the relative isolation of pioneer living.

While Millburn served many families from the eastern side of Lindenhurst, Angola was too far west to serve all but a few from the area. Thus, Lindenhurst has its own predecessor: the Sand Lake Post Office. Established on May 4th, 1863, the creation of Sand Lake reflected the growing number of farm families in need of services throughout the Lindenhurst area. Nestled between Hasting's Lake and Sand Lake, the Sand Lake Post Office included a school and cemetery as well as a mail stop. Presently, the Sand Lake Cemetery on Grand Avenue (IL Route 132) is one of the last vestiges of this early pioneer settlement.

SAND LAKE
ONE ROOM SCHOOL HOUSE
BUILT AROUND 1850

The Sand Lake School House
(Lindenhurst Village Archives, courtesy of Joyce Dever)

It is difficult to ascertain what the people of Sand Lake were like, as 19th century census records of the area were collected on the basis of township boundaries, not post offices. In these records, Lake Villa Township did not even exist, and the Lindenhurst area was split between Antioch and Avon Township. Luckily, early Lake County historian and founder of Hainesville Elijah M. Haines compiled extensive data on households in the area for his *Past and Present of Lake*

County, Illinois (1877). From these data one can get a partial glimpse of the Sand Lake community during the 1870s.

Taxpayers and Voters for Sand Lake P.O. Illinois, 1877

Antioch Township		Avon Township	
Name	Occupation	Name	Occupation
Beaty, William	Farmer	Burnett, J.B.	Farmer
Fiddler, Chris	Farmer	Burnett, A	Farmer
Hall, Frank	Farmer	Douglas, I.M.	Farmer
Leith, Samuel	Unknown	Day, Melvin	Farmhand
Miller, Henry	Farmer	Davis, Thomas	Farmhand
Spring, Henry	Farmer	Fenlon, Vilotte	Farmer
Sherwood, H.S.	Bricklayer	Ibester, John	Farmer
Sherwood, Stephen	Bricklayer	King, William	Farmer
Stewart, Alex	Farmer	King, James	Farmer
Stewart, J.J.	Farmer	Kendall, George	Farmer
Stewart, Robert	Farmer	Kendall, G.W.	Farmer
Stewart, A.H.*	Resort Owner	Kingsley, William	Farmer
		Lester, Henry	Farmer
* Stewart operated		Leinen, Michael	Farmer
the Lakeside Water-		Leinen, John	Farmer
ing Place, one of the		Manzer, Timothy Jr.	Farmer
earliest large resorts		Manzer, Timothy Sr.	Farmer
in the area. The		Manzer, L.C.	Farmer
Watering Place		Quinn, Jno.	Farmer
would eventually be		Smith, A.M.	Farmer
sold to E.J. Lehmann		Smith, Mrs. Ellen	None recorded
and become the		Thompson, E.A.	Carpenter
Lake Villa Hotel		Thayer, G.E.	Farmer
		Thayer, Henry	Farmer
		Woodward, Charles	Farmer & Postmaster
		Wright, H.L.	Bricklayer
		Wright, G.A.	Farmer
		Woodward, Jno.	Shoemaker
		Wright, S.A.	Farmer

It is not surprising perhaps to find that the primary occupation was farming. A few other residents contributed through the necessary skills of brick-baking, lay-ing, and carpentry to the community. Charles Woodward agreed to be Postmaster when not tending to his farm.

Frank G. Hooper, early postmaster (Lake Villa District Library Archives)

With no train or major roads through the area, isolation defined life around Sand Lake. Diaries and oral histories reference the difficult journey to Waukegan—a major point of trade and goods by the 1870s and only a few miles away. Early settler Christopher Manzer died in an 1845 snowstorm on journey back from Waukegan. Chicago travel provided even more obstacles. A diary entry from Herman Hall (sexton, carpenter, and relative of Frank Hall) reveals the difficulty of travel to and from the big city as late as 1884.

THE WHITE FARM, AVON TP LAKE CO. ILL. RES. OF Wm EMMETT, ESQ. OF CHICAGO.

The White Farm on Sand Lake, or "Emmett's Place"
(Lake Villa District Library Archives)

Hall departed on Monday, August 25th from the Monaville post office. As he did not have his own horse, Hall hitched a ride with area postmaster Frank G. Hooper (relative of B.J. Hooper). This was a common practice, but it meant Hall could not travel directly to Waukegan; rather Hooper took him through the local postal route, which at that time included Monaville, Sand Lake, Millburn, Gurnee, and Waukegan. By the time he had arrived in Sand Lake, it was late so Hall stayed the night at an acquaintance's house known as the White Farm. In his journal Hall remarks "put up at Emmit's (sic) house for the night." The next morning Hall finished his journey to Waukegan, and he took the 9:01 a.m. train into Chicago. After staying the night in Chicago (he attended a meeting of Civil War veterans), he missed the 3:00 train back to Waukegan, and so he had to catch the 4:10 train instead. On Thursday he spent the morning in downtown Waukegan waiting to find a ride. Luckily, Hooper was making his Thursday return to Monaville (via the postal route). It took Hall a total of four days to make the journey to and from Chicago.

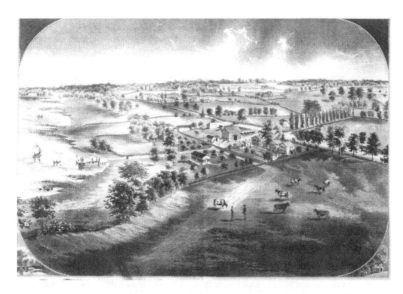

Stewart's Lakeside Watering Place (Lake Villa District Library Archives)

The story of A.H. Stewart points to the future of the region. Neither a farmer nor a carpenter, Stewart was one of the few wealthy landowners of Sand Lake. The source of that wealth was his resort, the Lakeside Watering Place, which sat on his 300-acre gentleman's farm, Stanwood, and capitalized on the beauty of the area's lakes. His success in the tourist business was mixed, foremost because the natural beauty of the region had to compete with the relative difficulty of travel to this remote outpost of Chicago. By 1883, Stewart had sold the farm acreage and resort to Ernst Johann Lehmann, a wealthy Chicago business man and department store mogul. It would be Lehmann who would fix the problem of the region's isolation—he would bring the train.

2

Grand Resorts & Clean Ice

Two Problems, One Solution

When Ernst Johann (E.J.) Lehmann purchased the Lakeside Watering Place in 1883, he had a dual vision for the area's greatest asset: the lakes. Throughout the fringes of Chicago (and into southern Wisconsin) a growing resort industry was meeting the needs of Chicago's middle and upper class citizens. Those who could afford a chance to get out of the stale city air flocked to the prettiest examples of the Midwest countryside; they came looking for relaxation and restoration through nature. This was especially true during the humid summer months, when relief from the city was most needed. Many husbands would send their families to these resorts and, after a week of work in Chicago, would ride the train to meet them for weekend fun.

LAKE CITY

Late Stewart's Farm, is the

MOST POPULAR SUMMER RESORT

IN THE NORTHWEST.

It is located among the Hills, Valleys, and Lakes of

LAKE COUNTY, ILLINOIS.

Only Two Miles from Fox Lake, Eight Miles from Gurnee and
Forty Miles from Chicago.

The LAKE CITY HOTEL and surroundings have been arranged, regardless of expense, for the accommodation and comfort of guests, with commodious cottages, which will be rented either furnished or unfurnished during the season. Lake City presents more Picturesque Scenes, Romantic Ravines, Historic Hills, Beautiful Lakes, Lovely Lawns, Mammoth Oaks, and more extensive Hunting and Fishing Grounds, than all the other advertised resorts combined.

E. J. LEHMANN, Proprietor.

WILLIAM STANHOPE, Manager,

P. O. Address: STANWOOD, ILLINOIS.

Branch of

Lake City Hotel,

GURNEE, ILLINOIS,

Is located at Gurnee Station, forty miles north from Chicago, on the Chicago, Milwaukee & St. Paul Railway. Gurnee Station is the principal junction of the railway and stage lines connecting Chicago with Lake City, Fox Lake, and the chain of lakes which form the great health and pleasure resorts and hunting and fishing grounds of the Northwest. Guests will find ample accommodations, while the charges will be reasonable at all times.

Branch of LAKE CITY HOTEL,

Fox Lake, Lake County, Illinois,

Is located on Fox Lake and its rivers, being about ten miles from McHenry, Ill. Boats run daily from McHenry to Fox Lake, stages running daily from Fox Lake to Lake City, a distance of not quite two miles, over a mountain country.

P. S.—Going to McHenry is fifty-eight miles from Chicago, on the Chicago & North-Western Railroad, thence by boat to Fox Lake.

E. J. LEHMANN, Proprietor.

WILLIAM STANHOPE, Manager, Stanwood P. O. Lake County, Ill.

An advertisement for the Lake City Hotel
(Lake Villa District Library Archives)

E.J. Lehmann planned a similar retreat among the lakes and hills of the area. He renamed Stewart's resort Lake City Hotel and by 1885 had established a post office of the same name near the present day corner of Route 83 and Grand Avenue (the Sand Lake post office had closed on July 14th, 1882). The name Lake City had already been claimed by another Illinois town, however, so Lehmann changed the name of both the resort and the post office to Lake Villa. Both names were calculated to paint a clear picture in the minds of would-be tourists. To overcome the problem of travel to the Lake Villa Hotel, Lehmann established a reliable stage coach service between Waukegan and Fox Lake. He even opened two smaller hotels in Gurnee and Fox Lake to give the resort crowd maximum flexibility in their travel.

These efforts would not be enough. Though the money to be made from resorts was substantial, there were two persistent problems. First, stage coach service, no matter how reliable, could not compete with the resorts directly situated on rail lines. Second, the resort business closed up in the winter; the Lake Villa Hotel could not be a year-round operation, though it would require year-round maintenance.

To solve the first problem, E.J. Lehmann determined to bring the train to Lake Villa. Throughout the 1880s, there had been an expectation that any rail line through the region would pass through the unincorporated post office of Monaville. This did not serve Lehmann's ambitions, however, and by 1885 construction began on the Wisconsin Central Rail Line through Lake Villa. Despite the dismay of Monaville's residents, by 1886 Lake Villa had fully operational train service to and from Chicago. Whatever other coercion Lehmann may have used, it is clear from land records that he sold the necessary lumber and land to Wisconsin Central for one dollar. Monaville would disappear from the maps by 1900.

Wisconsin Central train, Lake Villa Depot
(Lake Villa District Library Archives)

The arrival of train service also gave Lehmann a solution to his second problem. Part of Chicago's success in the meat packing industry had been the result of ice cars on trains. Packed into these large ice boxes, Chicago exported vast amounts of meat to wherever the rails could take it. While these ice cars were a great boon to Chicago's economy, they required clean ice to be effective. Ice without impurities, sediment, or pollution stays frozen longer, making it the choice for transport over long distances. Unfortunately for Chicago, most of its available lake and river ice was relatively polluted by ship traffic and industrial waste. Meat packers throughout Chicago began to compete for access to the most economical source of clean ice in the region: country lakes.

The Consumer Company Ice House (Lake Villa District Library Archives)

Once Lehmann had secured a rail line, Lake Villa could join the region's ice-cutting economy. Ice houses were set up on Cedar Lake, on Crooked Lake, and (two) on Deep Lake (the Knickerbocker and the Consumer). There was even a modest operation on Sand Lake, most likely run by William and Robert Emmett's White Farm. In the winter, ice cutting operations brought migrant workers from the city (they replaced the resort crowds who were headed back to the city) and kept the Lake Villa and Sand Lake region busy throughout the year.

The Wealthy Arrive

E.J. Lehmann's business venture was a resounding success. The Wisconsin Central train service that began with four daily passenger runs in 1886 expanded to fourteen runs by 1910. The Lake Villa Hotel became a vast resort complex; it included a bowling alley, dance hall, gambling casino, several cottages, and over 150 rooms in the main hotel building. Lehmann gave discounted room rates to his hundreds of Fair Store employees during lulls in the tourist season, making certain that the resort buzzed with activity from spring until autumn.

E.J. Lehmann's Lake Villa Hotel c. 1900
(Lake Villa District Library Archives)

Before refrigeration technology replaced ice car trains in the 1920s, the ice cutting industry helped the region, but especially Lake Villa, grow rapidly in population and business. Lake Villa itself was incorporated as a village in 1901, and by 1913 the Lehmann's (with the help of the politically connected resort manager John Stratton) had successfully lobbied the state government for the creation of a separate Lake Villa Township. By all measures, Lake Villa was a thriving outpost of the Chicago's growing metropolitan economy.

What effect did this boom have on the Lindenhurst region? Though many stopped at Emmett's Sand Lake White Farm and Resort on their journey between Waukegan and Lehmann's resort, the Lake Villa train cut down on Grand Avenue traffic. By the time Sand Lake students helped write the region's 1918 history, "... nothing remain[ed] at the present to show of the once beautiful White Farm." In many ways, the area remained quiet and agricultural. Students continued to attend Sand Lake School, the Bonners and others tended their farms, and life in general moved at a country pace.

Nevertheless, subtle changes were taking place. Though E.J. Lehmann did not live to see the full success of his resort—his wife Augusta sent him to a New York Sanitarium (under suspicious circumstances) in 1890 where he died a decade later—his family did. The Lehmanns had six children survive into adulthood:

Edward John (also an E.J.), Otto W., Ernst E., Emelie W., Augusta E., and Edith M. Though these privileged children spent much of their childhoods in Chicago, they also grew up playing in and around the Lake Villa Hotel. It is no surprise then that all of them eventually developed property in the area. Edward John purchased the property just north of the hotel and built Longwood Farm (the still extant Lehmann Mansion), Otto W. built Chesney Farms to the west (where the modern day subdivision Chesney Shores currently exists), and Ernst E. purchased 240 acres of Sand Lake property to the east. The estate was lined by two rows of Linden trees and so named the Lindenhurst Farm.

Ernst E. Lehmann's Lindenhurst Farm-Main Estate
(Lindenhurst Village Archives)

The Lindenhurst Farm was just as grand as the other Lehmann estates throughout the area. A brief description of the farm comes from the local 1918 history:

> One of the prettiest spots in the town of Lake Villa is "Lindenhurst Farm," the home of Mr. E.E. Lehmann on Sand Lake. The farm itself occupies some 240 acres of land. The residence, which overlooks the Lake in one of its choicest spots, is constructed in the bungalo (sic) style, with several long low porches overlooking the water. The exterior is white with a stained roof of green, as are all the buildings. Surrounded by a mass of beautiful shrubbery, green lawns, and graceful elms the house is barely visible from the road, but on entering the drive, one sees the beauties of the rose garden, the fish pond, the pergola, and the flower garden. A lane of silver maple trees adjoins the farm, leading to the

Fowler farms, across the lake, and this adds to the picturesquesness (sic) of the place. Near the approach to the house is the garage, a pretty little building, wrapped in green foliage, and to the right of this are the dog kennels.... On the opposite side of the road [Grand Avenue] are the tenant houses, the main barn, a smaller one where the bulls are housed, a large wagon house, creamery, ice house [eventually the site of the Lindenhurst Civic Center], and milk house.

According to the *1917 Prairie Farmer's Reliable Directory of Farmers and Breeders in Lake County* Lindenhurst Farm was primarily a dairy farm, specializing in Guernsey Cows. Ernst E. ran the farm in a meticulous fashion; dairy workers had to wear all-white uniforms (including gloves) and cleanliness was of the utmost importance. When not tending to his milking operation, Ernst's other passion was raising his prize-winning Pekinese dogs. The kennels on the property were quite extensive and had their own separate maintenance and operation staff.

By the first decades of the 20th century, the Lehmanns were not the only prominent family in the area. The beauty of the region had not been lost on E.J. Lehmann's wealthiest hotel guests, and by 1910 some built their own country estates. The Peacock family (still famous for their jewelry) settled on Deep Lake and Crooked Lake. Emelie Lehmann married into the Peacock family after meeting in the area. Many older residents recall life in the area with these privileged families. Otto W., Edward J., and Ernst E. brought many wealthy friends to the region during the hot summer months, though according to many, they often did not mingle with the working class farmers.

Perhaps the most profound consequence of this boom was the vision it created. Interest in developing more resorts and summer cottages to capitalize on the region's natural beauty came quickly after the Lehmann success. In one instance, a series of developers and speculators laid claim to a particularly scenic area just south and west of Sand Lake and the Lindenhurst Farm. The new development was named Venetian Village. Between 1926 and 1929, Nathan Hale Engle & Sons—a Chicago-based realty and construction company—began developing a unique subdivision of summer cottages with Italian themed streets nestled between three lakes. According to news articles, the average price for these modest homes was $700, though additional amenities could push the price closer to $1000. After only three years, the Great Depression brought building to a halt; it would remain this way for a decade. By the time construction recommenced in 1940, N. H. Engle & Sons had taken full control of Venetian Village's 450 acres. According to local historian Karen Loftus, Engle proclaimed Venetian Village the "Beauty Spot of the Lakes Region."

Unfortunately for Engle's sons (Morton, and the twins Edward and Willard), the social trends and economic forces that had made the Lake Villa/Sand Lake region a popular, turn-of-the-century resort destination had mostly fallen away by 1940. A decade of high unemployment followed swiftly by the Second World War made the summer cottage an unattainable (and even distasteful) luxury for many. Refrigeration technology financially ruined the local ice-harvesting operations. Venetian Village began as a resort but could not be completed that way, and Morton Engle knew it. His new vision for the area would be far removed from the grand resorts that had populated the lakes region since E.J. Lehmann's arrival in 1883. Engle would bring a distinctly 20th century version of the American Dream to the shores of Sand Lake: the suburb.

3

Mort's Vision

Original Lindenhurst Estates sales brochure
(Lindenhurst Village Archives)

We Invite You ...

To visit one of America's most beautiful lake estates ... Lindenhurst, for many years the private estate of one of Chicago's leading families. Now ... it has been added to famous Venetian Village, long one of Chicagoland's outstanding home developments.

Combine the beauty and scenic grandeur of 3 spring fed lakes, the advantage of country living with city conveniences in a location that was chosen by millionaire families for their own comfort and enjoyment and you have Lindenhurst Estates addition of Venetian Village.

—Original Lindenhurst Estates sales brochure, c. 1952

18

Ernst E. Lehmann, millionaire owner of the 500-acre Lindenhurst Farm and Estate was dead by 1930. A larger man, E.E. was often intense and demanding. He took pride in his Pekinese and his dairy operation, but did not have the easy demeanor and good-natured mischievousness that made his brother Otto so well loved. Otto was also more fortunate in love; he married his brother Ernst's first wife C. Affeld in 1907. Ernst had only been married to her for three years.

The sale of Lindenhurst Farm to close family friend Edna Siebel after Ernst E.'s death marked the end of an era. If E.J. Lehmann's six children had loved the area, their children did not. Drawn to the glamour of Chicago or to the promise of the east coast among other American aristocrats, E.J. Lehmann's grandchildren did not stay long. By 1955, the whole Lehmann family had left the area, with the exception of Edward John's wife Florence who refused to sell her beloved Longwood Farm. It remained in the family until her death in 1964. The Lindenhurst Farm would not remain with family or friends; Edna put the farm and all 500 acres back up for sale by the late 1940s.

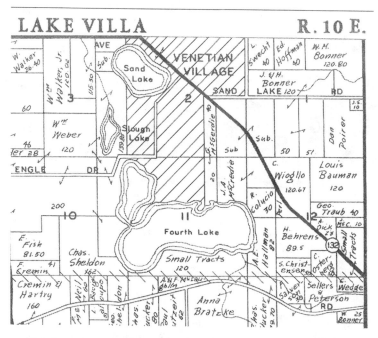

P14: Avon Township 1954: Showing N.H. Engle & Sons Lindenhurst addition to Venetian Village. The addition would not remain a part of Venetian Village for long. (Lake Forest College Archives)

Nathan Hale Engle's son, Morton, seized the opportunity. After a decade of successful development throughout Venetian Village (and its western extension—the newly christened West Miltmore) the sale of E.E. Lehmann's estate represented the potential doubling of land held by N.H. Engle & Sons. Morton Engle (or Mort) had come back from a tour of duty in the Army excited to take on the family business. By 1952, the grand Lindenhurst Farm was being subdivided; the first homes were finished by the fall of 1953. The original subdivision's boundaries included Fairfield Road and Hazelwood Drive in the west, Sprucewood Lane to the north, Ironwood Drive and Magnolia Lane to the east, and Greenbriar Lane just south of Grand Avenue. In addition to modern curvilinear streets (relatively rare north of Lake Forest and the North Shore), Lindenhurst Estates boasted modern homes that would contrast favorably with the older resort structures in the area. Engle, mixing practicality with consumer appeal, began draining and repurposing marsh land and sloughs to create Lake Linden and Waterford Lake for both drainage and recreation. Lake Linden is a perfect example. On a 1939 aerial map of Lake County, one can clearly see the recognizable wetland outlines of the future Lake Linden, as shown in the 1974 aerial map.

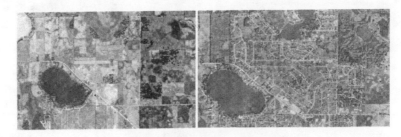

Aerial maps of Lindenhurst: 1939 and 1974
(Lindenhurst Village Archives)

The Lindenhurst Estates addition to Venetian Village was born. The overall effect was a very modern, if somewhat isolated, residential development. Whether he knew it or not, Mort Engle was to be the beneficiary of a great shift in American culture: automobility.

This is not an undeveloped community, you are not pioneering, you will become a resident of one of Chicagland's most ideal suburban communities. Here you will find thousands of people living near fine schools, churches, shopping centers, and movies. You can enjoy a new lease on life, women find relief from city smoke and soot, children enjoy clean, healthful country air without the hazards of dangerous city traffic, and men can add years to their life through the enjoyment of gardening, fishing, hunting or just plain loafin' in the country. Yes, it's hard to believe all these grand advantages can be yours and within daily commuting or driving distance of Chicago.

—Original Lindenhurst Estates Sales Flyer, c. 1952

After World War II, the United States found itself once again in possession of a roaring economy. It also faced the dilemma of crowded and deteriorating cities (a decade of economic crisis had taken its toll) coupled with an influx of newly married veterans looking for homes. The solution was the automobile. Though the car had been wildly popular since the first decades of the 20th century, roads had not kept up with the American enthusiasm for the roadster. National automobile registrations paint this picture. In 1945, registrations were estimated at 25,800,000. By 1956 (the year of Lindenhurst's incorporation), the number had reached 54,300,000; automobiles on American roads had more than doubled in little more than a decade.

Until the 1940s, Chicagoland roadways consisted of numerous small paved roads criss-crossing many smaller, unpaved roads. Rain or flooding frequently washed out muddy lanes. Traffic regulation was scarce and little heeded. Accidents were common and likely fatal—owing more to unsafe vehicles than to speed. The automobile was a milestone of human invention, but the automobility that sprung from the faster, safer, multi-lane highways of the 1950s was a revolution.

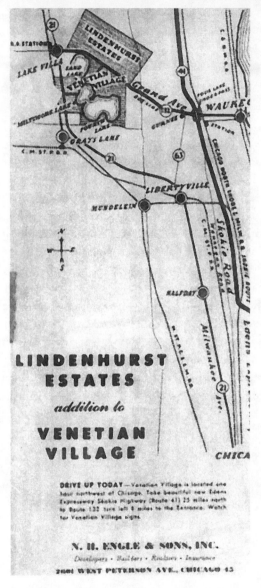

A map to Lindenhurst Estates—notice the absence of the toll way
(Lindenhurst Village Archives)

Much as the steam locomotive destroyed notions of time and space in the 19th century, modern highways and expressways repeated the process in the middle decades of the 20th. The heaviest automobile traffic in Northern Lake County moved from Chicago and along the Lake through the North Shore into Waukegan and through to Milwaukee. Out of a desire to relieve congestion and improve travel times, state and local authorities shifted, expanded, and repaved Old Skokie Road from Wisconsin to Glenview. Upon its completion in 1951, the Edens Expressway Skokie Highway (Route 41/94) brought Chicago to Lindenhurst's door. The six-hour, unpredictable, and hazardous drive from Chicago to the countryside became a boring but dependable hour-long commute. Before, there had been a clear distinction between the two sides of American life: the city and the country. A person lived, worked, and shopped in the same place. In theory, this new automobility allowed a person to work in the city and live in the country. In practice, city dwellers desired the freedom and benefits of the country but with the comforts of city life. Mort Engle's new suburban addition to Venetian Village struck a perfect balance between these desires. Lindenhurst Estates would be so successful that by 1956, it would become more than a subdivision; it would become its own suburb.

Advertisement for a Lindenhurst Estates starter home c. 1953
(Lindenhurst Village Archives)

Meet the Neighbors

Who were the original buyers who came to call Lindenhurst their home? In the mid 1950's, the baby boom reached its height, and young families with children (or plans to have them) moved to the area in droves. These first residents often worked in Chicago or the near Northwest suburbs. George and Helen Skelton are a good example. Early residents, they were both civically minded. Helen Skelton would become one of the first village trustees, as well as the first President and founding member of the Lindenhurst Garden Club. For George, the reality was a daily commute to the ornamental railing firm he owned in Chicago. Despite the commute, the charm of Lindenhurst proved too much to ignore.

An early aerial view of Lindenhurst Estates streets—note the street names
(Lindenhurst Village Archives)

The desire for affordable but modern housing had been well met by the post-war boom of suburban development near Chicago's city limits, but Lindenhurst Estates added the charm of country living. One unnamed, original resident puts it this way:

> In the early days of Lindenhurst it seemed the "best of both worlds," country living—two beautiful, historic towns (Millburn and Lake Villa)—a fast easy drive to Waukegan to board the Electric North Shore Train, which ran to the Chicago Loop.... No toll way yet, and we never had to lock our doors when we left the house. Everyone was a "newcomer."

Mort Engle's homes were another draw to the subdivision. Neither prefabricated nor shell homes, the original houses boasted birch flush floors, carports, fully installed septic tanks, and very modern General Electric Gun Type Oil Furnaces. (Some residents remember the roof being optional, though.) Lots and homes were purchased very quickly, and the roster of early residents continued to expand: Skelton, Flanagan, Fabry, Lewis, Parpan, Randall, Henderson, Behrendt, Ringstmeyer are but a few.

Perhaps Lindenhurst Estates grew too quickly. Four short years after Mort Engle first subdivided the Ernst E. Lehmann property, the young residents began clamoring for greater control over zoning, population, and ordinances. Without these controls, the pioneers of Lindenhurst Estates feared that the community they had grown to love would change too rapidly, and in the wrong direction. Automobility and quality home construction had brought these people from Chicago to the country, and they were not about to give up their "best of both worlds." The solution was incorporation.

4

The Village of Lindenhurst

General Petition No. 13773

Lindenhurst Estates successfully wedded the modern suburb to the countryside far north of Chicago. This unique character drew residents who were naturally bolder, willing to be involved, civic pioneers. The early families were happy about the subdivision's growth but eager to maintain the positive qualities of the subdivision that had brought them to Mort Engle in the first place. Unfortunately for the residents, only incorporated villages, towns, and cities could exact the kind of local control (through zoning, ordinances, allocation of government funds, etc.) necessary to make sure Lindenhurst Estates would develop in an orderly fashion. The only incorporated village in the township was Lake Villa, and that had occurred over fifty years prior. Certainly, it would be rare for the incorporated subdivision (The Estates) of an older unincorporated community (Venetian Village) to seek local autonomy—even rarer considering Lindenhurst Estates was less than three years old.

But, autonomy is exactly what these pioneer families desired. By 1956, a group of community leaders had retained attorney Ellis Fuqua, of the Waukegan law firm Fuqua & Fuqua, to move forward on the incorporation of Lindenhurst Estates. The community, however, did not want their new village named like a subdivision. Residents had long since dropped the "Estates" when referring to their community, so the filings related to the process of incorporation used the community's common name: "Village of Lindenhurst."

Ellis Fuqua, Lindenhurst's first attorney (Lindenhurst Village Archives)

Mort Engle supported the endeavor, and he allowed use of his real estate office (Woodland Realty) for the petition and legal work. With his support, and many hours of work, these active residents were able to get their wish. State General Petition No. 13773 begins this way:

> This matter now coming on for further hearing upon a petition and affidavits filed herein and upon the returns of the Judges and Clerks of Election upon the statement of the special proposition election held September 29th, 1956 at Engle's Real Estate Office, Grand Avenue, Lake Villa [Township], Illinois the territory hereinafter specifically described of the vote on the questions of organizing and incorporating said territory under the general law as the "Village of Lindenhurst" …

The proposition on incorporation of September 29th was a success. In a March 1981 letter from Ellis Fuqua himself, he recalled that the proposition received 139 proper signatures. Lindenhurst Estates was gone; in its place, the first new

Lake County village in years. A new order was attached to General Petition No. 13773:

> IT IS ORDERED AND DIRECTED that an election be held within said Village of Lindenhurst on Saturday, the 15th day of December, 1956 between the hours of 6:00 o'clock A.M. and 5:00 o'clock P.M. Central Standard Time ... for the purpose of electing village officers for the said village, pursuant to law.

Work began in earnest. The community had less than two months to organize an election for their first officials, who had been set as follows: one village president (sometimes unofficially referred to as Mayor), six village trustees, one village clerk, and one police magistrate. Morton Engle once again offered the various buildings of the old E.E. Lehmann estate for functions relating to the election. Ellis Fuqua proved invaluable in dispensing legal advice, and in securing official election supplies (which at the time cost $12.50). The village would have their election on schedule, December 15th, 1956.

SPECIMEN BALLOT

Special Election for Village Officials

VILLAGE OF LINDENHURST

Polling Place: Engle's Real Estate Office
Grand Avenue, Lake Villa
Lake County, Illinois.

SATURDAY, DECEMBER 15, 1956

Minard E. Hulse

County Judge of Lake County
and Judge of the County Court
of Lake County, Illinois.

FOR VILLAGE PRESIDENT
(Vote for One)

☐ FRED BELLER
Beck Road

☐ LOWELL GRAVES
Briar Lane

☐ CARL M. LARSON
Old Elm Road

☐ LEE R. LEWIS
Woodlane Drive

Top of ballot from Lindenhurst's first election, December 1956
(Lindenhurst Village Archives)

Lindenhurst would have a small government, so it needed to be effective. The irregular timing of the December special election meant that a new, second election would be mandated just four months later, in April 1957. This, however, did not stop potential candidates from signing up for the December elections. As one might expect, the energetic citizens turned out a long ballot that included many of the village's earliest residents. By the end of the first election, the village board had been elected, and Lee Lewis became Lindenhurst's first village president.

Lindenhurst: The Early Years

According to one 1956 news article, "meetings of the Village Board will be held on Saturdays because most of the members are commuters and get home late." There was no permanent structure for theses meetings, so Helen Skelton—an original trustee—hosted the first one in her home on Fairfield Road. The village board held subsequent meetings in other trustees' homes until Engle offered use of the old Lehmann milking parlor, complete with porcelain walls.

In April of 1957, Lindenhurst held its first full-term election. By an overwhelming majority, residents (now numbering nearly one thousand) elected candidates from the newly formed Citizen's Party of Lindenhurst. An April 1957 issue of the *Grayslake Times* reported, "Mayor Bob Randall, elected to office [of village president] in April 18th, 1957—heading the Citizens' Party which swept to victory at every turn, in a flood of straight ticket balloting." This new village board, however popular, had a real problem: it would be one full fiscal year before Lindenhurst would be able to collect on levied taxes.

The residents, business leaders, and President Robert Randall's new government would have to work together. The board could only appropriate so much money without going into debt, but there were real needs in the village—like a squad car; light poles for the quieter, darker streets; and expensive, but essential for a commuter community, snow removal services. Lindenhurst's first full village budget tells the tale. The village board and Police were voluntary; specialists' salaries only reached $1600 collectively. Concerning village expenses, fully one-fifth of the budget was devoted to buying one squad car (including maintenance). All told, the 1957 budget for Lindenhurst totaled 13,335.00. Here is a closer look at the budget:

1957 Budget, Section 1. That for the purpose of defraying all the necessary expenses and liabilities of the village of Lindenhurst for the fiscal year commencing May 1, 1957, and ending April 30, 1958, the following sums, or so much thereof as by law may be authorized, be and the same are hereby set aside and appropriated for the following purposes, to-wit:

Village Positions, 1957	Salary	Top Five Village Expenses, 1957	Cost
Village President	None	1. Squad Car (plus radio, oil, gas,	
Village Trustees (6)	None	& repair)	2300.00
Village Clerk	None	2. Surfacing of Streets	1500.00
Village Treasurer	None	3. Construction & Maintenance of	
Village Marshal and		Drains	1000.00
Deputies	None	4. Village Legal Fees	1000.00
Village Attorney	600.00	5. Police Supplies	8830.00
Village Engineer	500.00		
Health Officer	100.00	All Other Village Expenses	5105.00
Building Inspector	400.00		
Total of all Village Salaries, 1957	1600.00	Total of all Village Expenses, 1957	11735.00

How did the village get this money? According to the accounts of original residents, everyone chipped in. John Slove ran a committee to raise the money to defray the expense of Lindenhurst's legal fees and squad car, while other business owners were asked to help bring street lighting throughout the village. At the main intersections of Grand Avenue—Granada Boulevard and Sand Lake Road—stop signs were needed in addition to the streetlights; the cost was thirteen dollars.

If financial difficulties were an issue, they were no match for the enthusiasm of community leaders. By 1958, Thor Neumann had brought Lindenhurst its first business (located near the present-day CVS pharmacy)—Thor's Shell. Furthermore, Mort Engle had always had plans to develop a shopping center for his Venetian Village addition. Those plans took on additional momentum with support from the vast majority of the community. These young families wanted convenience in their countryside setting.

An early rendering of B.J. Hooper School (Lindenhurst Village Archives)

That same year, President Randall brought to fruition a long-standing desire of residents: a neighborhood school of their own. Though Sand Lake School (District 48) had served the area since the 19th century and the days of the Sand Lake Post Office, it had been closed as a school and sold to private owners by 1952. Furthermore, the Millburn school district could not meet the needs of Lindenhurst's growing population. As a board member of Lake Villa School District 41, Randall hoped for a modern school for Lindenhurst. Mort Engle's original Lindenhurst addition did not include land for a school, so Randall haggled with the long-settled Bonner family to annex a parcel of farmland adjacent to Lindenhurst's eastern border. The school was named after School Board President and Rexall Pharmacy owner Bert J. Hooper. In October of 1958, the brand-new B.J. Hooper School opened its doors to Lindenhurst children.

By the end of the 1950s Lindenhurst had become one of the most successful and rapidly growing suburbs of the Chicago area. Furthermore, the energy that had marked the first decade of the village would continue unabated. An article from the November 14, 1957 *Grayslake Times* is telling:

> Residents of Lindenhurst (although many men commute to jobs in Chicago and elsewhere) are highly civic minded. They have organized service and social clubs for adults and active organizations for children of all ages—it's a community of young people eager to do things. No one says 'Let George do it'—George doesn't have a chance in this bustling community. With that type of attitude there's only one way to go—forward! No wonder that Randall can smile despite his battle with the headaches of a young community.

The commentary captures both the potential and the pitfalls of civic-mindedness. Though the early years were a model of community effort, this did not always translate into agreement. Along with the hard work of the village came disagreement and politics. These "headaches of a young community" would test a series of village governments, and their citizens.

5

The Fight for "Lindy"

CAREFUL, LINDY. CHECK THE INGREDIENTS!
THINGS AREN'T ALWAYS
WHAT THEY SEEM TO BE

NEW ANNEXATION BEING CONSIDERED

"LITTLE LINDY LINDENHURST,"
a young lady with growing pains
and a lot to learn has offered
to use her womanly wiles to
call to your attention matters
of concern to you and your
village. We hope you will
enjoy her little adventures.

Conservative-Progressive Party newsletter c. 1958
(Lindenhurst Village Archives)

Little "Lindy" Lindenhurst

"A young lady with growing pains and a lot to learn has offered to use her womanly wiles to call to your attention to matters of concern to you and your village." In many ways, Little "Lindy" Lindenhurst symbolized the difficult political problems present at the beginning of incorporation. The village had always been advertised as a careful mix of country living and modern amenities. This balance was not always easy to maintain, however, and residents did not always agree on how to achieve it.

Starting with the election of President Randall in 1957, influential residents began to side with local political parties on the most contentious issues. Newsletters were the parties' method of choice for communicating to Lindenhurst's residents, and they offer a fascinating glimpse into the growing pains of the village. While political fighting rarely became hostile, a look back at this material reveals the central issues important to the young, civic-minded members of the community.

The Citizens' Party had early successes. As the party of Randall, they swept into all areas of village government in the 1957 election. Broadly speaking, this party advocated greater growth for the village, believing that it could only benefit the community. As of 1959, many small businesses had expressed interest in leasing space in the proposed shopping center, but as yet no large anchor store had committed to the project. New residents, however, would increase the tax base and make the center more attractive to a larger business.

President Randall also wanted to bring businesses and community organizations to the village. He had been instrumental in purchasing land from Engle to build St. Mark Lutheran Church. President Randall often worked closely with Mort Engle, who had continued to acquire nearby land from retiring farmers and resort owners. By the end of the 1950s, Engle possessed 550 acres adjacent to the north and east boundaries of the original village; he believed the time was right give more people an opportunity at Lindenhurst living. He even had a name for this new addition: Seven Hills.

Engle, however, had not yet worked out all of the kinks that came with Lindenhurst living. Geographically, widespread wetlands, marsh fields, and sloughs had always marked Lake Villa Township. When E.J. Lehmann brought the Wisconsin Central Rail Line through Lake Villa in 1886, the project was almost abandoned because of a pernicious sinkhole just south of the town. Mort Engle was aware of the challenges to residential building on this low, wet landscape; he, in fact, did much to combat this condition during the construction of Lindenhurst Estates. The clearest examples of this are the original manufactured lakes of Lindenhurst: Lake Linden, Waterford Lake, and Potomac Lake. Aside from their recreation value, these lakes were necessary to fight potential flooding due to heavy rains.

"HURRY, DADDY, AND I'LL TAKE YOU OUT TO YOUR CAR!"

Conservative-Progressive Party newsletter, c. 1959
(Lindenhurst Village Archives)

Engle's precautions mostly worked. Some residents, however, were treated to occasional flooding that ruined gardens, entered basements, and even churned up septic tanks. Septic tanks were another problem. Lindenhurst's relative isolation from other modern communities meant that there was no city sewer system in place. While the tanks worked most of the time, it is not difficult to imagine that some Chicago transplants were less than pleased to suffer this very "country" concern. For these residents it became more important to have sewer and drainage upgrades in the *existing* village than to expand onto Mort Engle's Seven Hills.

Paradoxically, these residents were joined politically by those fearful of losing the quaint character of Lindenhurst to unrestrained growth. For them, the key reason for incorporation in the first place was to control growth in the village. Many felt uneasy about such a large addition to Lindenhurst. Would the developers maintain the high standards of the original village? How would the government cover the additional cost in roads, snow removal, and emergency services?

Out of these disparate issues the Lindenhurst Conservative-Progressive Party was born. With Randall's Citizens' Party in full control of the village board, matters had moved smoothly and with little controversy. By May of 1959, however, three trustee seats had been captured by members or sympathizers of the C-P Party. Their subsequent newsletter thanked all who had helped the party win these contested seats. Alex Bartling (Chair of the Road Committee), Georgia Matthies (Chair of the Building and Grounds Committee), and Charles Pawlowski (Chair of the Licenses and Ordinances Committee) were determined to bring strong debate to the Citizen's Party over the issue of annexing Seven Hills.

That summer and fall, each party's newsletter waged a war of words against the other regarding the future of Lindenhurst. The C-P Party noted, "[The village] must revise any annexation proposal to require any developer to install a complete storm and sanitation sewage treatment system adequate for any area to be annexed from the village." The Citizens' Party claimed that this represented an anti-growth stance that was harmful to the future of the village. The C-P Party shot back: "We support growth and annexation, but with village control. It is the contention of the C-P party that the ordinances we have are sub-standard to the present day needs." Furthermore, "The Lake Villa Fire Department now has difficulty locating any trouble spots in our village; adding annexed property would cause more problems.... What does this mean for your pocketbook?" The Citizens' Party, picking up on the last line, retorted, "What does it mean to *your* pocket book? The additional revenue would <u>decrease</u> rather than increase your taxes."

The debate came to a head on January 5, 1960 at a special village board meeting of the Planning Commission. The agenda: to decide on the annexation of Seven Hills. Supporters of both parties were in attendance, and the mood was tense. As the Board debated the pros and cons of doubling Lindenhurst's size, President Randall stood up and demanded to know who had written the last Conservative-Progressive Newsletter, which sharply criticized the Citizens' Party. Trustees Bartling and Pawlowski said they did not write the newsletter but endorsed it, while Trustee Matthies said she had been unaware of the newsletter's contents until she had received her copy in the mail. Mort Engle was in attendance that night with his wife, Catherine, who often attended village meetings. He asked those in attendance to support the future growth of the village. When questioned about the condition of village septic tanks and flooding concerns, he responded quickly, "Persons with septic systems have to learn to use them. They won't stand the same load that city sanitary systems take." When it seemed that there might not be a consensus on the issue, Engle offered one more piece of information: if Lindenhurst were to annex Seven Hills, Piggly Wiggly (a major grocery chain) would be interested in anchoring the Linden Plaza shopping center.

VILLAGE VIEWS

Volume 8   MAY, 1960   No. 5

SHOPPING CENTER FOR LINDENHURST

A newspaper headline regarding the proposed shopping plaza
(Lindenhurst Village Archives)

It was decided; Lindy would be for expansion. A Lindenhurst shopping center had been the decisive factor to many residents moving from the city. If the Seven Hills addition would help the realization of that dream, then the consensus was growth. The annexation was approved, and despite some continued opposition (notably from Pawlowski), Lindenhurst added 550 new acres of residential homes, lakes, and parks. The new village boundaries expanded past Grass Lake Road to the north and east closer to Millburn.

This would be the first of many political struggles. Mayor Theodore "Ted" Flanagan replaced President Randall in 1961. (The state government had dropped the term Village President; it has since been reinstated.) Flanagan held this office for over two decades—except for a single term won by Mayor Admiral French from 1965 to 1969. Flanagan dealt with many issues during his tenure. He oversaw the building of a dedicated village hall and the expansion of municipal services. Mort Engle made further attempts at village expansion, some successful, others not. In 1974, the village board held a particularly heated debate on the merits and drawbacks of building a high-density development on Sand Lake.

Many women were also involved in political skirmishes. Luella "Lu" Stanley (village treasurer, clerk, and trustee throughout the 1960s) ran a tough, but ultimately unsuccessful, bid for Mayor in 1969. Records indicate that even when not serving the village in an official capacity, she often wrote honest and critical letters to local newspapers to stir community debate.

Lindenhurst Party political flyer c. 1983 (Lindenhurst Village Archives)

In 1983, another political sea change occurred when Trustee Robert Ratch and his Lindenhurst Party slate of candidates waged a tough, three-way campaign against Mayor Flanagan and hopeful Phyllis Lucas. Ratch won the election, and his party filled many seats on the village board, effectively ending the Flanagan

Era. Mayor Ratch had his own share of struggles, including a protracted fight with Lake Villa Township over the location of a new Fire Department substation and emergency facility—all in an attempt to maintain the high quality of Lindenhurst public services. He also brought new roles to village government. The board debated the merits of hiring a village administrator for efficient and effective operation of the growing government; ultimately, the village added the position. When Mayor Ratch left office in 1991, he had created a thoroughly modern village government.

In the last decade and a half, Mayors Paul Baumunk and James Betustak have overseen a new era of rapid geographical expansion and explosive population growth. This has included keeping the village commercially attractive in the face of Gurnee Mills, a major area shopping center, and balancing the proliferation of new subdivisions with the need to bring new services to village residents. The role of the village board has become far more complex since incorporation, very different from the fight over Mort Engle's 550 acres.

And yet, forty years later, the Seven Hills conflict stands as a symbol for the many controversies and difficult decisions that the village of Lindenhurst has faced over the past fifty years. The desire for forward growth and progress, carefully checked by the high standards of residents, has become the mark of most village decisions. These political fights should not necessarily be viewed in a negative light. In many ways, they represent a level of involvement in local affairs that has always been typical of Lindenhurst's energy and desire to stay active in the maintenance of their treasured community.

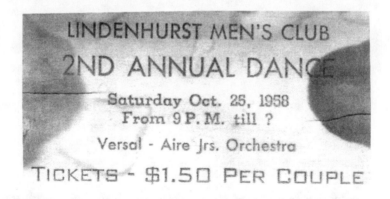

Lindenhurst Men's Club fundraiser ticket (Lindenhurst Village Archives)

The Unity of Civic Spirit

Politics are just one manifestation of civic life. The Lindenhurst Garden Club, the village Welcome Wagon committee, the Lindenhurst Men's Club, and the Lindenhurst Women's Club were all early thriving civic associations. Many residents have found community service opportunities through their churches, while others have worked to preserve parks and lead environmental clean-up efforts. Still other community leaders volunteered their time and energy in the service of the village's children. Well-supported Little League Baseball teams, chapters of the Boy and Girl Scouts, and the creation of Lindenhurst Days (re-envisioned as Lindenfest in 1983) all exemplify this tradition. Since the 1980s, the introduction of an independent Lindenhurst Park District has only strengthened the mission to provide young and old alike with a chance to join with other residents in work and play. Lindenhurst's many examples of local associations, clubs, and leagues testify to the vigor with which village citizens participated in shaping their community.

Women's Club Meeting: passing of the presidency c. 1960
(L to R) Mary Zanck, ____, Lu Stanley, Lois Flanagan, Grace Slove
(passing the gavel), Betty Ireland, Dorothy Verdick
(Lindenhurst Village Archives)

At the center of Lindenhurst, civic life has been the Lindenhurst Men's Club and the Lindenhurst Women's Club. Charged with no narrow purpose, these civic organizations have held fundraisers for village improvements and services, organized dances and shows to provide entertainment choices, and helped in any way they could benefit the community. Both the Men's and Women's Clubs were formally created in 1957 (though residents had been volunteering and organizing community activities since the beginning of Lindenhurst Estates.) Doug Sanders, the first Men's Club President, laid out his vision for the organization:

> The object of the club shall be to cultivate by personal acquaintance, closer relations between neighbors, to bring about greater understanding between neighbors, to encourage unselfish devotion of time, thought, and effort to the advancement of the village of Lindenhurst, to offer inspiration to the youth of Lindenhurst, to promote the best interests of the people of Lindenhurst, to aid and abet the government of the village of Lindenhurst in its lawful duties; to promote, sponsor and assist in all manners of youth activities, to bring about good fellowship and understanding with neighboring communities, and to accomplish the adoption of sound policies for the welfare of the community.

The Women's Club began as an auxiliary to the Men's Club, open primarily to the wives of its members, but by January of 1960 it had become an independent organization open to all of the women in the village. This crucial step, bolstered by the club's first president, Grace Slove, made certain the Women's Club would not be overshadowed by the Men's Club.

The future home of the Lindenhurst Men's Club
(Lindenhurst Village Archives)

The Lindenhurst Civic Center on Old Elm Street (later renamed the Thor Neumann Civic Center) is perhaps the most symbolic gift of the Lindenhurst Men's and Women's Clubs. Prior to 1960, these clubs had met in a variety of places, but most often at the American Legion home and remaining buildings of the Lindenhurst Farm. The community worked together to secure labor, material, and funds for a modern addition to the Lindenhurst Farm Ice House. The clubs raised approximately $50,000, and work began on the building. Though originally intended for the Lindenhurst Men's and Women's Clubs, it soon became apparent that the building fulfilled a great community need. In 1976, Karen Loftus wrote,

> ... The Lindenhurst Civic Center was planned as a clubhouse for the Men's Club, when their first meeting place was torn down. However, the scope and proportions of this building grew into [a variety of] village activities. The Civic Center is put to good use for Scouting activities, teenage and adult club meetings, card parties, style shows, dances, rummage sales and other fund raising activities....

After almost fifty years of community service, the village had outgrown the Lindenhurst Civic Center. New park district facilities and the expansion of other opportunities for Lindenhurst residents helped close the historical Center. The building was sold in 2006.

The Thor Neumann Civic Center
(Lindenhurst Village Archives, photograph by Joyce Dever)

The first Lindenhurst Garden Club officers were elected on June 3rd, 1957; Helen Skelton was president. In many ways, the success of the Garden Club speaks to the desire of early residents to practice and perfect "country" habits. The Club's early notes often refer to master gardener Alfred Sokolies and his wife Edeltraut. Sokolies gave residents gardening tips because according to some "most of us 'city folk' are novices at gardening." The Club often held garden shows (Lois Flanagan won Best Rose Arrangement at the 3rd Annual Show), traveled to regional shows, and ran fundraisers for the Civic Center and Countryside Hospital. Members also helped with community beautification. When Mort Engle donated Willow Park to Lindenhurst, the Garden Club designed the landscaping. Moreover, in 1960, the club was involved in the original floral work for the new Linden Plaza.

The Lindenhurst Bicentennial Parade (Lindenhurst Village Archives)

Even Lindenhurst's young were given the opportunity to participate. Generations of Lindenhurst youth have been involved in all manner of sporting activities, offerings that have greatly expanded over the decades. The American tradition of Little League Baseball found a receptive home in Lindenhurst. Its youth soccer program began earlier and has been more successful than many similar programs across the suburbs of Chicago. Such leagues have required untold hours of volunteer service from residents. The forest preserves and many parks of

Lindenhurst have been developed with an eye toward the village's youngest citizens as well. In addition, the Lindenhurst Civic Center has served as a base of operations for Boy Scouts and Girl Scouts meetings and events, as well as countless other teen functions. Even in the earliest days, when resources were scarce, residents found ways to provide youth recreation; community leader Mike Fidanzo offered his basement and hi-fi stereo for dances (most likely at the suggestion of his own teen-aged daughters.)

Community involvement has been at the heart of Lindenhurst's first fifty years. When the Conservative-Progressive Party of Lindenhurst developed Little "Lindy" Lindenhurst as a symbol of political activism over forty years ago, they were also giving birth to the idea that a community can be more than houses and businesses, streets and sewers. She is the spirit of Lindenhurst, something to be protected, cherished and even defended. Though residents have not always agreed on what was best for the village, it is enough to say that they have always agreed to want the best.

6

A Booming Village

A billboard promoting the future Linden Plaza
(Lindenhurst Village Archives)

The "Malling" of America

The Skokie Road/Edens Expressway may have helped Lindenhurst get its start in 1951, but its effect on the village did not compare to the 1958 completion of the six-lane, Lake County branch of the Tri-State Toll Way (I-94). At the time, downtown Gurnee was east of the toll way, and Lindenhurst was the first incorporated village due west. A new arterial road meant transit to and from Chicago was even easier, and it became easier still to leave Chicago for good. All over the country the process of leaving the city for the suburb, which had begun in the middle of the 20th century, continued unabated throughout the 1960s, 70s, and 80s. Chicago was no exception. Census data reveal a dramatic story. In 1930, seventy-six percent of the 4.5 million people living in the six-county region (Lake,

Cook, DuPage, Will, Kendall, and McHenry counties) lived within the borders of Chicago. By 1960, that percentage had dropped to fifty-seven; by 1990, Chicago's population represented only thirty-eight percent of all people living in the collar counties.

The tidal change in living patterns was only part of the puzzle. The pioneering residents of Lindenhurst had still mostly worked (and shopped) in or near Chicago. Throughout the sixties and seventies, industrial and white-collar businesses sprang up around the metropolitan area. Efficient expressways and improvements in shipping made this transformation viable. Further, service sector businesses realized the enormous potential of bringing shopping and entertainment opportunities to the suburban consumer. As some historians have dubbed it—the "malling" of America. Hawthorn-Melody Farms in Vernon hills was transformed into Hawthorn Mall; tellingly, Lakehurst Mall was built on the western outskirts of Waukegan, the declining center of commerce for northern Lake County. By the 1990s, the draw of far northern Lake County made the gargantuan Gurnee Mills project a reality, putting all number of conveniences at the doorstep of Lindenhurst's residents. The potential for growth in a village such as Lindenhurst was now without limit.

Lindenhurst Plaza's final phase of construction, 1960
(Lindenhurst Village Archives)

Luckily, Lindenhurst was prepared. By 1960, it was clear that the village had chosen a policy of growth. After just four years of incorporation, the village population had reached approximately 1200. By 1970, the population had more than doubled, reaching over 3100 residents. As Lindenhurst continued its rapid pace of growth throughout the eighties and nineties, current census figures place the village at approximately 15,000 residents. This growth wrought substantial changes in both the diversity of the community and the opportunities available to residents. The first major change, by most accounts, was Engle's new shopping center, Linden Plaza.

Governor of Illinois, Bill Stratton (Lindenhurst Village Archives)

Linden Plaza and the Growth of Commerce

In 1960, N.H. Engle & Sons development of Lindenhurst's Seven Hills addition was progressing smoothly, and the final phase of the village's shopping center was nearly completed. The village had advertised in newspapers and on billboards in search of interested businesses. If successful, the shopping center would ease residents' tax burden as well as draw more families to the village. Interest in the project went beyond area residents—Governor of Illinois Bill Stratton had flown in from Springfield by helicopter to view the center's progress. Governor Stratton's own history with the area is intriguing; his grandfather was John Stratton, one of E.J. Lehmann's closest business associates and the first Lake Villa Township Supervisor in 1913.

When Mort Engle had announced Piggly Wiggly's interest in becoming an anchor store, the project rapidly came together. By October, the new Linden Plaza opened for business. Four stores (not including the already extant Thor's Shell Gas and Service Station) comprised the Plaza's original tenants: Village Laundry, Linden Cleaners, Slove's Country Charm Bakery, and the Piggly Wiggly Grocery Store. The grocer fulfilled its purpose: to draw people to the Plaza. At 20,000 square feet, parking for sixty cars, and land available for eventual expansion, Linden Plaza needed desperately to become commercially viable. The store's variety helped—primarily a grocery store, the original Piggly Wiggly also housed a shoe department, an expansive home and garden department, and a full delicatessen service.

John Slove at work in his bakery (Lindenhurst Village Archives)

John Slove, an early local leader, was a community favorite. As village trustee, he ran successful fundraisers benefiting the all-volunteer police department. The result of his hard work was dramatic: an additional squad car with radio and a fund to "pay" officers a small wage for their service. Therefore, his bakery was a welcome addition to Linden Plaza. People from all over the township patronized the bakery. Slove, however, was no newcomer to the business. He already owned a successful bakery on Diversey Avenue in Chicago; the Linden Plaza just brought him nearer to home.

In the end, there was no need to worry about the plaza's success. By far the largest shopping center in Lake Villa Township, it fulfilled a need for convenience and served as another community-meeting place. Within the short span of a few years, an addition brought a barber shop—founded by Jim Nikolai and continued under John Miller; both pillars of the community, a pharmacy, a Ben Franklin five-and-dime store, and a billiard hall. By 1965, the popular Dog & Suds drive-up diner occupied the eastern end of the Plaza. Though Lindenhurst already had its first community physician in Dr. Jindrich Laurich, whose offices were housed in a building from the old Lindenhurst Farm, the plaza's second addition included a professional services building, where the first dentist Dr. T.E. Restarski, and physician Dr. Torres could practice.

The Linden Plaza before the expansion of Eagle Foods
(Lindenhurst Village Archives, courtesy of Joyce Dever)

After 1970, the commercial development of Linden Plaza and its surroundings greatly increased to meet the needs of the growing community. The plaza not only gained new tenants, such as Ellie and Herbie Schmidt's Flower Hut, but subsequent additions housed the original R.J.'s Eatery, Chandler's Fitness, Chinese and Mexican restaurants, shoe repair and eye care shops. Thor's Shell was torn down in the early 1980s to make room for an expanded grocery store as Eagle Foods replaced the Piggly Wiggly.

Development spread out from the plaza as well. Using a pamphlet titled "Is This Your Opportunity?" Mort Engle sought to sell the main estate of E.E. Lehmann's Lindenhurst Farm. Engle offered the building for purchase as a remarkable single family home, motel, or sanatorium for the price of $65,000. On three remaining acres, the home boasted a large patio, pergola and gardens overlooking the lake, eight bedrooms, a library, and multiple recreation rooms. Though it was never again to be used as a residence, the structure did house a restaurant and a nursing home before it burned down. Today an expanded R.J.'s Eatery resides on the property, though remnants of the original landscaping along Sand Lake remain.

The White Hen / 7-11 convenience store replaced the Dog & Suds and Cindy's Chicken, a fast food restaurant, opened on the south side of Grand Avenue. James "Jimmy" Streicher's Texaco Station initiated development of the intersection of Sand Lake Road and Grand Avenue. Later, he would sell the land directly to the east of his service station—it would eventually hold a smaller plaza and a McDonald's fast food restaurant. Jimmy maintained his service station until 1997, when he retired from the business. The original station was torn down, but the property presently houses a modern Mobil station. West of Linden Plaza, banking, real estate, and insurance companies, and more recently a restaurant, a funeral home, and car repair services have complemented the plaza's growth. Further west, Victory Lakes Care Facility became the village's biggest employer—and generator of tax revenue. By 1990, Lindenhurst's commercial growth was the most successful in the township, if not the region.

A newspaper article on John Slove's Country Charm Bakery
(Lindenhurst Village Archives)

The village's embrace of business has not waned. In recent decades, commercial expansion has come along Lindenhurst's borders. Waterford Commons brought business to Grass Lake Road. Victory Lakes opened a massive residential facility in 1998 to enhance and diversify their services. By the end of the decade, the village's attention turned solidly to the potential of a major commercial corridor along Route 45. Ironically, this corridor may some day overshadow the original plaza, which in countless ways has fueled Lindenhurst's expansion.

Serving the Community

The tremendous growth of the village brought an expansion of Lindenhurst's commercial base and necessitated a considerable widening in the scope of available community services. Police, fire, and rescue services were enhanced, while school and village government buildings were expanded and updated. Improved sewer systems and the development of a dedicated sanitary district helped meet the demands of the people, while an additional water tower represented the village's continuing growth.

Lindenhurst Village Hall groundbreaking ceremony, March 1974 (holding shovels) Judy Kempher, Ted Flanagan (back row left to right) Douglas Getchell, Al Ott, Fred Fabry, Dennis Powell, Don Henderson, Robert Ratch, James Johnson (Lindenhurst Village Archives)

By the 1970s, the original Lindenhurst Village Hall was poorly suited to the task of running a village; so, when this building burned to the ground, government offices were temporarily moved to Linden Plaza's professional building. Mayor Theodore Flanagan quickly made plans for a modern village hall just east of the Sand Lake Road and Grand Avenue intersection. After a groundbreaking ceremony in March of 1974, the building, which included a large maintenance garage, was finished in less than a year. For the next two decades Lindenhurst's Village Hall would house the government, police department, and after further additions in the 1980s, a post office sub-station.

The influx of families to the area put great pressure on the township's schools. Though a part of Lake Villa Consolidated District 41, B.J. Hooper School could not contain the growing population of students. Initially the school consisted of eight classrooms, a community room, a kitchen, and offices. By 1961, at just three years old, two additional classrooms were needed. Further additions to the school in 1976 and 1988 helped the district keep pace with enrollment, and a major renovation in the late 1990s brought school facilities up to date.

Another expansion of public services resulted from the desire of residents to increase the number of parks and recreation activities offered by the village. Mort

Engle's 1987 decision to donate his last 66 acres in the village for a park may have spurred the community to act. It was the passing of an era. Mort Engle had once owned over 200 acres of the town and now, over thirty years later, he had decided to give his last property back to the village. Mayor Ratch and his village trustees explored various ways to best expand park services. In 1988, these efforts culminated in the creation of an independent park district. Today, the Lindenhurst Park District maintains approximately twenty parks and offers a great number of seasonal activities.

Lindenhurst Police Department—Chief of Police Ron Coles sits second from the left, front row (Lindenhurst Village Archives)

The original Lindenhurst Police Department consisted of one village marshal and eight officers. All were volunteers and for the first decade, most improvements and acquisitions came from fundraisers and local donations. Officers supplemented this generosity by purchasing their own uniforms and phones when necessary. In 1963, the department added one full-time officer position (this was necessary to prevent Lake County's Police from taking over jurisdiction of the village). By 1971, Lindenhurst police were making a wage of $2.50 an hour. Long-standing Police Chief Ron Coles kept emergency response times low—he would later go on to be Lake Villa Township Supervisor. By the 1990s, the police force had outgrown their home in village hall and planning began on a separate Public Safety Building for the department. The new facility opened in 1999 under Chief of Police Jack McKeever's leadership. Originally seeking the priesthood, Chief McKeever ultimately settled on another vocation. He has spent over fifteen years serving Lindenhurst residents.

Problems also came along with rapid growth. The complicated history of village fire and rescue services provides one example. Unlike the police department, Lindenhurst has shared its fire and rescue services with both the village of Lake Villa and unincorporated Lake Villa Township, creating one Fire Protection District. While service has generally been excellent, the best location of services has caused many struggles between these three political bodies. Further complicating the issue is the Lake Villa rail line. The district's fire station is on the west side of the tracks, while the rescue station is on the east side. Long freight trains often close the tracks for minutes at a time, and many residents have debated the impact on emergency service as a result. The many battles in the late 1980s between Mayor Robert Ratch and members of the Fire Protection District mentioned in the previous chapter are a particularly notable illustration of this debate.

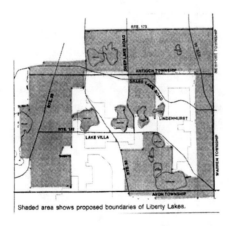

Shaded area shows proposed boundaries of Liberty Lakes.

Boundary map of the proposed municipality Liberty Lakes, 1986
(Lindenhurst Village Archives)

The village has even managed to fight off what was perhaps the greatest threat to any future growth: Liberty Lakes. Born out of a fear of annexation by Lindenhurst, Lake Villa, and Round Lake Beach, concerned citizens of Lake Villa Township drew up a plan to create their own incorporated village. In a meeting during the autumn of 1986, the planners named their proposed village Liberty Lakes. This was an appropriate name, as leaders Jo Garrett and Ronald Geer believed they were freedom fighters against the high cost of taxes and the higher cost of forced municipal improvements that came with incorporation into existing villages. Because the goal was to band together all unincorporated pieces of Lake Villa Township, the resulting boundary of Liberty Lakes was an odd and fantastic patchwork that included over 24 square miles and almost 9,000 residents. Some were sympathetic to the cause, such as Township Supervisor Dorothy Thompson. Most, however, were not. Lake Villa Mayor Joyce Frayer and Mayor Ratch joined forces to fight what they labeled a monster—Liberty Lakes' success would completely encircle Lindenhurst and forever doom any chance of growth. After a year of argument and a series of heated legal battles, the question of Liberty Lakes' incorporation found itself in front of the Illinois Supreme Court. In December 1987, the ruling came: Liberty Lakes was dead. Subsequent attempts to bring Liberty Lakes back to life have never come to fruition.

Lindenhurst has done much to expand and improve community services over the past fifty years. In concert with the village's commercial growth, these improvements have helped the village continually draw new residents to the area, while keeping long time residents satisfied with the community. By the end of Mayor Ratch's tenure, the village of Lindenhurst represented a fully mature municipality, with professional services and an enviable commercial base. More impressively, the great expansion of the village had not hurt the village's small-town charm. The pressure to grow, however, would not stop, and it became increasingly apparent to both residents and the village government that the balance between future growth and country living would become harder to maintain.

7

A Balancing Act

The Balance

Mayor Robert Ratch's vision had been a success. At a September 2000 village meeting, he recalled how he had withstood the pressures of "development at any price." His goal was to bring the village quality homes and access to the area's natural beauty, while preserving opportunities for the village's future commercial expansion. Upon his retirement in 1991, the village of Lindenhurst had over 8500 residents, a fully functioning park district, and an average home valuation double that of the township's other incorporated village, Lake Villa. He had joined forces with Lake Villa to fend off the growth-constricting Liberty Lakes, and plans were developing for the renovation and expansion of the Lake Villa District Library.

For all of its positives, the Ratch legacy also left Lindenhurst with a great responsibility. The pressure for growth would not abate, nor would residents' desire for ever greater village services. This responsibility was left to the Mayor Paul Baumunk and his village trustees. Known as a peacemaker, the charismatic mayor had his own vision for Lindenhurst. In a March 1995 *News Sun* interview, during his reelection campaign, he stated: "The most important thing for bringing Lindenhurst into the 21st Century is a vision on growth and development … and also to be able to keep Lindenhurst's unique 'rural' identity." The mayor and his government would spend the next decade maintaining a delicate balance of progress and growth for the village, while keeping a commitment to concerns of natural preservation and village tradition.

The Bonner Farmstead today
(Lindenhurst Village Archives, photograph by Joyce Dever)

Farming in Suburbia

Tractors had always fascinated Howard Bonner; his father preferred farming on a horse. The one consistent facet of Bonner family farming had always been the land. For over 150 years, various Bonners (all related back to Scottish immigrant William Bonner) farmed the land along large portions of Lindenhurst's eastern border. Howard "Shorty" Bonner had kept up the family's tradition of grain and dairy farming. However, Shorty Bonner was also a civic leader; he held positions in various civic organizations such as the Millburn School Board and the Lake Villa Fire Protection District. His family had given Lindenhurst the land to build B.J. Hooper School. But the land never changed.

Until 1995. "At 76, it's time to slow down a bit." Shorty, after well over fifty years of farming, had no children or grandchildren who wanted to continue the Bonner tradition. Shorty's children had bowed out of the family business as early as the 1960s—though the farm remained operational. Nevertheless, Lindenhurst's meteoric growth created more conflict with every passing year; farming in suburbia had become difficult. According to Shorty's interview with the *Pioneer Press* in June of 1995, the situation had become "frustrating for both the farmer and the neighboring homeowners. 'Kids make forts or ride mini bikes through the farm field damaging crops.' Bonner says he chases them out every summer, but there's a new group every year."

If encroaching suburbia had worsened resident-farmer relations in some ways, it had also created an excellent opportunity—land wealth. As northern Lake County grew in population, the demand for new housing starts increased as well. The general result has been a strong upward trend in the price of land, particularly when near to established villages with dependable public services. The farm that no Bonner would work after Shorty's retirement would be put on the market.

Westfield Homes quickly drew up a plan: 525 homes (a mix of single-family units, town homes, and duplexes) on winding streets with a connection to McDonald Woods Forest Preserve. When the developer brought the plans to the Lindenhurst Village Board in January of 1995, most were supportive save one problem: the name. Westfield Homes had chosen the name Fawn Run. Trustee Carol Zerba believed it was "too cutesy." Mayor Paul Baumunk put it more bluntly: "It's just not a Lindenhurst name; it sounds like a place where you kill baby deer." After a series of changes, the village board formally annexed the Bonner farm into Lindenhurst and gave its approval to Westfield Homes' master plan. Ultimately renamed Country Place, development on the new subdivision began with an important question unanswered: what to do about the old Bonner farmstead?

The Village and the Developer

The fate of the Bonner farm, while of historical importance, was not a rare challenge for the village of Lindenhurst. Throughout the 1980s and 90s, subdivision developers had flocked to northern Lake County like gold rush speculators. The mix of inexpensive and plentiful open land (relative to Chicago) and well-established communities created the perfect economic environment for rapid village growth. Subdivisions such as Farmington Green and Harvest Hill on the east side of the village, Mallard Ridge and Sedgewood Cove on the west side are but a few examples. Lindenhurst continued to expand not only in terms of population, but also in land area.

This same story has been played out in municipalities throughout Lake County, but Lindenhurst has held its developers to higher standards of aesthetic quality and preservation of open space. One clear example is the proliferation of village parks. Throughout the 1990s, Mayor Baumunk and the village government consistently challenged developers to donate significant land for new neighborhood parks. The philosophy behind this was simple: it is a privilege to develop residences in Lindenhurst, so developers should be willing to go beyond in providing amenities for any new subdivision. At times, this has caused conflict. Throughout the 1990s, the village board closely monitored development to ensure the village-approved plans matched what developers built on the ground. Generally, the village has grown without sacrificing quality, which has benefited the whole community.

Lindenhurst has not been untouched by the headaches of rapid growth. One notable crisis occurred in the early stages of the Auburn Meadows subdivision on the northwest side of the village. By 1996, early homebuyers in the subdivision faced problems with flooding, and some even had liens against their homes due to the developer's financial difficulties. Janet Brandess, developer of the subdivision, came before the village board to address these issues, but ongoing homeowners' complaints marred attempts at a solution. In the end, another developer was brought in to alleviate the residents' problems and finish the project. As late as 1999, the village halted Town & Country Builders from continuing the Falling Waters project, a mix of residential homes and an industrial park on the Route 45 corridor, after residents brought forth concerns of significant structural problems in existing phases.

Some challenges have involved Lindenhurst's incorporated neighbors. As northern Lake County's population soared, growing pains drew villages ever nearer, forcing serious discussion and sometimes-tense debate over future annexation of unincorporated land and permanent borders between existing incorporated villages. To the north and west, Lindenhurst forged agreements with both Antioch and Gurnee on the future of each one's municipal boundaries. A long tradition of shared township services made boundary negotiations with Lake Villa especially critical. In many ways, the two sister communities forged workable solutions to most problems and strengthened an already close relationship. In one notable example, Lindenhurst opened its chamber of commerce to Lake Villa business: the result would be the creation of the Lindenhurst-Lake Villa Chamber of Commerce and Lindenhurst's financial support for the recreation of Lake Villa's 19th century train depot. The station marked the 1996 return of commuter rail to the township.

These clear agreements among villages did not always work, however, and annexation has not always been welcome. In late 2000, Mayor Baumunk and the village made the difficult decision to annex forcibly the last unincorporated parcels of land on the western side along Route 45 between Grass Lake and Sand Lake Roads. These parcels gave Lindenhurst full control over land west of Route

45, but the move was controversial because much of the property belonged to the extended Bonner family, Bernie and Jane Webber. Mayor Baumunk carefully defended the move: "This may not be popular with homeowners, but we must make decisions for the future of the village." At the source of the trouble was Lindenhurst's other neighbor to the east, Old Mill Creek. Unlike negotiations with Gurnee, Mayor Baumunk could not secure any agreements with Old Mill Creek to respect traditional eastern boundaries. The village board feared an incorporation attempt across Route 45 by Old Mill Creek would jeopardize current and future plans to develop the roadway's commercial potential.

Despite the problems of village development and annexation, Lindenhurst's embrace of responsible growth has yielded much for the community. It is, however, just one piece of village's identity. If the 1990s were a decade of tremendous growth for Lindenhurst, it has also been a decade of preserving and reclaiming the village's natural beauty.

The McDonald Woods Forest Preserve (Lindenhurst Village Archives)

The Legacy of Preservation

One of Lindenhurst's principal charms had always been its manufactured lakes. Unfortunately, by the 1980s a combination of run-off, sedimentation, and invasive fish populations had significantly lowered the quality of the lakes. Piecemeal attempts to combat these problems met with varying degrees of success. It was with this problem in mind that Mayor Baumunk and various other concerned residents helped create the Lindenhurst Lakes Commission. The goal of the commission was far from simple: to reclaim the lakes in an environmentally sound way for the enjoyment of all residents, and to maintain the lakes' effectiveness as drainage basins and village flood control. The Mayor and the village board chose Bill Roesler, a former television channel ABC-7 cameraman, to be the first commissioner. As a resident of Lindenhurst, Roesler had fallen in love with the lakes. In an August 2005 *News Sun* interview, and after a decade as Lindenhurst Lakes Commissioner, Roesler recounted the village's successes in restoring the lakes to an almost pristine condition.

The village has nurtured its trees as much as its lakes. In the 1990s, Kenneth Anderson and the Lindenhurst Plan Commission led the charge to ensure existing trees were protected from infestation and aggressive development while continually plant new trees. Anderson took his dedication a step further by training to become a certified arborist for the village. In 1998, the village's work had paid off; Lindenhurst was designated a Tree City as part of the Tree City USA program, a national effort to recognize communities that support the protection and maintenance of trees.

Some preservation efforts have been led by collaboration between village and county officials. The Lake County Forest Preserve has had much success in purchasing land for open space within and near the village. The 225 acres of woods and wetlands donated by area realtor Arthur B. McDonald are a prime example. Notable for the meandering ravines more typical of Lake Michigan coastline, McDonald Woods were preserved in 1974 according to McDonald's wishes. Overall, Lake Villa Township holds the most acreage of preserved land in Lake County excepting those townships along the Des Plaines River.

The Country Place subdivision (photograph by author)

The Lake County Forest Preserve was also instrumental in deciding the fate of Shorty Bonner's farmstead. In June of 1995 Bonner, Westfield Homes, Lindenhurst, and the Lake County Forest Preserve worked out an arrangement that included easement trading and a sizable payment for Bonner. Lake County Board member (and township resident) Suzi Schmidt wept tears of joy; fellow board member and Chairperson Robert Depke had agreed to allocate county funds to preserve many of the farm's existing structures and to convert the property into a Lake County Heritage museum. The Bonner legacy had been saved for succeeding generations.

The Bonner family-opening ceremony for the Bonner Heritage Farm
(Lindenhurst Village Archives)

Still, some ways of life can never be fully saved. When asked about the county forest preserve, Shorty said he remains suspicious. His 1995 interview reveals why: "The forest preserve annoys Bonner with what he calls their 'fancy names' for its acquisitions. Fourth Lake Fen should be called slough and Rollins Savannah should be called woods—because that is what they are." It may be a well-taken point coming from Bonner, but "slough" and "woods" are the words of a pioneer past. Lindenhurst is a developed and modern community, far removed from its agrarian days. In place of *slough, woods,* and *farmstead,* contemporary residents use terms such as *Country Place, Mallard Ridge,* and *Auburn Meadows.* These subdivisions may recall an earlier time, but they can never fully restore it. Hence, Lindenhurst's ever difficult balancing act: between future and past, growth and preservation.

8

Epilogue

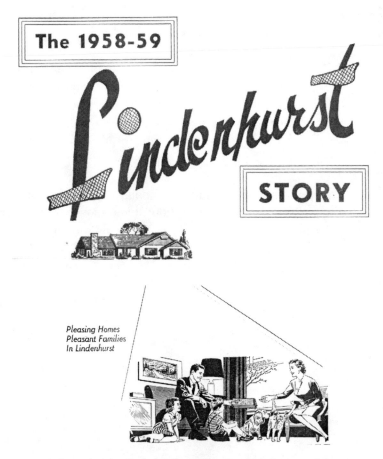

An early advertisement for the merits of Lindenhurst living
(Lindenhurst Village Archives)

"The Lindenhurst Story"

Lindenhurst continues to thrive in the 21st Century, and much of its success can be described in one word—Civic. This word and its derivatives imply a whole host of ideals that have become the recurring theme of our village's history: volunteerism, kindness, dedication, service, betterment, and above all, community. In May of 2003, this community welcomed their seventh Village President and Mayor James Betustak. Like most of Lindenhurst's leaders, Mayor Betustak embodies the above ideals. Nevertheless, he is just one of many village residents who have spent years, even decades, dedicating both time and energy in the service of building a better community.

Achievements keep coming. The village has grown to over 14,000 people. The new Lindenhurst Community Center continues to expand. The heart of village commerce, the Linden Plaza, has undergone a well-deserved renovation. The recent opening of the Lindenhurst Center for Business will deepen the village's commercial base. On December 18, 2006, the much-awaited Grass Lake Road Fire Station broke ground, ensuring more effective service for those in the northern section of the village. The long-standing Victory Lakes health care facility, from the village's 1986 annexation on its western border, might soon expand to include a full-service 140-bed, hospital. Forest preserves, reclaimed lakes, and new parks—one aptly named Millennium, have enhanced the village's natural beauty.

In a nod to Lindenhurst's green thumb beginnings and in anticipation of its golden anniversary in 2006, Lindenhurst distributed four thousand bags of daffodil bulbs and designated the Golden Daffodil as its official flower-Village Resolution 05-09-1496, signed September 26, 2005. By January of 2006, the Illinois House of Representatives adopted House Resolution No. 722 enshrining the village of Lindenhurst as the "daffodil capital of Illinois." And on November 11, 2006 the Lindenhurst Veterans Memorial was dedicated to all those who truly define the word "Civic."

Lindenhurst Veterans Memorial, 2006 (Lindenhurst Village Archives)

December 2006 marked fifty years of pleasing homes and pleasant families in the village of Lindenhurst. There are many differences: Bonner's Farm hides under the lawns and sidewalks of a modern subdivision, the Lindenhurst Men's and Women's Club Civic Center only remains in memory, and Mort Engle can no longer dream up another addition to Lindenhurst Estates. Nevertheless, similarities persist: Bonner's homestead remains; after 40 years, Art Neubauer still monitors village funds; and from the corner of Grand Avenue and Lindenhurst Drive, one can imagine the layout of E.E. Lehmann's Lindenhurst Farm in its full rural majesty.

Celebration and reflection marked Lindenhurst's Golden Anniversary. The village filled the year with talks and multimedia presentations on village history, community gatherings such as the village sock hop, and dedications of remembrance to those who have contributed the most—the veterans. This book grew from this yearlong celebration, though it remains an imperfect tribute to the community's past. Lindenhurst's true history does not rest in the pages of this book, but rather in the faces of neighbors and friends—and the best tribute would be to continue building a better community for the fifty years yet to come.

APPENDIX

INTERVIEWS
LINDENHURST'S FOUNDING FAMILIES

The roots of local history find their greatest expression in the people who have lived it. While historical photographs pack the punch of immediately transporting the reader back to another time, the very fabric of historical narrative builds from the memory and recollection of community founders, long-ago residents, and current citizens. Though many of these voices have found their way into the preceding chapters, there are many others that did not. Some of these founding voices are so compelling, however, that it seems appropriate to include them in their own special section. What follows are excerpts from interviews of some of Lindenhurst's earliest residents conducted by members of the Lindenhurst Historical Committee; I present them here unabridged with light editing for clarity and context.

Note: Joyce Dever and James Streicher conducted the following interviews between July of 2006 and May of 2007. (Interview questions in bold print; interviewed resident's names in italics.)

Interview with Bob Bunkelman

When did you first move to Lindenhurst and how did you choose this area?

July 1, 1962—we wanted good schools.

What was it like when you first moved here?

There were many wide, open spaces.

What organizations were available and were you involved in them?

The Lindenhurst Men's and Women's Club.

What do you consider the biggest changes and when did they start changing?

The influx of people when sewers were put in [the village.]

What were the recreational activities?

The Civic Center—dances and parties and Little League games and activities.

Interview with Jim Nikolai

When did you first move to Lindenhurst and how did you choose this area?

1959—I was the first barber in the village—12 years in Lindenhurst.

What was it like when you first moved here?

The village was very beautiful and quiet. [The Linden Plaza] only had the bakery, Piggly Wiggly, and dry cleaners in shopping area. The winters were very harsh.

What organizations were available and were you involved in them?

The Men's Club and the VFW. We had many good times and everybody knew everybody else then.

What do you consider the biggest changes and when did they start changing?

When the sewers came in things started changing—right around 1970.

What were the recreational activities?

Many children joined the Boy Scouts and Little League.

What would you like to see happen in the future and what past things do you consider have been lost?

I would like to see more activities for the children other than the organized sports.

Interview with Ray and Pat Parpan

When did you first move to Lindenhurst and how did you choose this area?

We moved here in September 1956. We lived on Fairfield Rd. for five years and then built a home on Chestnut Circle.

What was it like when you first moved here?

Linden Lake was just a cow pasture. There were just about a dozen houses around here. This left plenty of room and open space for the kids to play.

What organizations were available and were you involved in them?

Ray was in charge of helping to form the Little League. After the Civic Center was built, we had an after school game hour for all the kids. What a job. When the Lake (Linden) froze, he cleared an area so the kids could play hockey at night. Jack Kemper installed lights and Bob Bunkelman was there to help. The Civic Center hosted dances every holiday and it was always packed—very different from today. The village was small and everyone knew everyone. It is too bad everyone works so hard today and there is little time for neighborhood fun. Our Women's Club put on card and bunko parties and fashion shows to raise money to keep the Center going. That is suffering now because of a lack of volunteers but times change and we must go with the flow. Also, Ray was President of the Men's club.

What do you consider the biggest changes and when did they start changing?

We saw the toll road built; it increased the population dramatically.

Interview with Dewey Royce

When did you first move to Lindenhurst and how did you choose this area?

September 7, 1961. I was in the Navy and wanted to settle down when I retired and when looking for a home, I liked the open spaces. I liked the school system and it was close by our house. My children, grandchild, and great grandchild have all gone to the same school. It was like living in the country.

What was it like when you first moved here?

Everybody had a septic tank and it was very quiet. The shopping area was the Piggly Wiggly, the bakery, and the Laundromat.

What organizations were available and were you involved in them?

I belonged to the Men's Club, the VFW, and the American Legion.

What do you consider the biggest changes and when did they start changing?

Too many houses once the sewers were put in.

What were the recreational activities?

Girl Scouts, picnics at Linden Lake. The most exciting thing in town was going to the Dog and Suds.

What would you like to see happen in the future and what past things do you consider have been lost?

I would like to see people friendlier with neighbors and more socialization.

Interview with Ken Slove

When did you first move to Lindenhurst and how did you choose this area?

1954—We started the bakery in December 1954—We had the 12th house in Lindenhurst. My Father had a bakery in Chicago before starting here, and he was the first tenant in Linden Plaza in 1960.

What was it like when you first moved here?

We have good memories. Everybody knew everybody.

What organizations were available and were you involved in them?

My father was the first Police commissioner, and he donated the first squad car. He was on the Sanitary District for Lindenhurst, and there was a lot of controversy when the sewage plant was going to be built; but he knew it was needed for growth in the area.

What do you consider the biggest changes and when did they start changing?

I rode through Lindenhurst recently and could not believe all the development. We used to hunt on Bonner's Farm for pheasant. We would always give half of the pheasants to the Bonners, and Mrs. Bonner would then fix a big dinner for all of us—great food.

What were the recreational activities?

Boys Club—we did not have formal activities. We always had a neighborhood baseball game and played basketball at B.J. Hooper. Ray Parpan would open the gym for us and chaperone the kids. He would always run laps around the gym and said the reason he did this is that when he played basketball in the school gym when he was a boy that the man that organized it would do this. He always said that he would do the same thing if he had the opportunity.

Interview with Jack Thompson

When did you first move to Lindenhurst and how did you choose this area?

December 1960. It was a young community and we wanted to be a part of it.

What was it like when you first moved here?

Lindenhurst reminded me of the days of pioneers, but it was also a quiet and friendly atmosphere.

What organizations were available and were you involved in them?

The Lindenhurst Civic Center and Men's Club. We were very involved the first week we moved into our house.

What do you consider the biggest changes and when did they start changing?

After the sewers, it brought in more people and homes and became a more congested community.

What were the recreational activities?

There were many: Little League, Men's Club programs and dinners, not to mention the Boy Scouts, Fishing derbies, and the Women's club.

What would you like to see happen in the future and what past things do you consider have been lost?

Would like to see more people involved in the clubs to have more of the programs and good times that marked the beginning of the village.

Also, let us know any stories that you would consider of interest about the community.

A big barn was the first Men's Club. The club held meetings where the Firestone is—the milk house was behind the barn. The bar in the Civic Center is the original icehouse. After eight years, Mort Engle gave the property to the Men's Club. He stipulated that it must be used for village people. We never had a lot of money to work with. Many of the park properties were purchased by buying up land that people were unable to pay the taxes. To pay the taxes some of the members made payments from their own pocket.
Ray Caldwell was the Justice of the Peace. The community was one big family. At the time, we felt like pioneers. The Civic Center was the social center—all functions were family affairs. We really had good times. People came for the open spaces, and it was so great being able to start a new town. Bonner's wife sold eggs door to door from 1960 to 1965.

Interview with Jim Walsh

When did you first move to Lindenhurst and how did you choose this area?

1965. We lived on the south side of Chicago at the time. We were looking for home on a lake and found Lindenhurst.

What was it like when you first moved here?

It was very blue collar and rural. We met many people that were looking for this same thing. A village that was close to Chicago and affordable with open space.

What organizations were available and were you involved in them?

The Lindenhurst Men's Club, Prince of Peace Church, and Little League baseball. I was involved in them all.

What do you consider the biggest changes and when did they start changing?

When the subdivision of Seven Hills began.

What were the recreational activities?

A nice summer day at Miltmore Beach was a day well spent. Also, a little boating on any of the nearby lakes.

What would you like to see happen in the future and what past things do you consider have been lost?

We have lost the small town feeling, and it never will be the same.

Interview with Norm Whitlock

When did you first move to Lindenhurst and how did you choose this area?

October 1958. Land was reasonable, and it was country living.

What was it like when you first moved here?

The Plaza started the year after I moved here, and I started working part time as a barber.

What organizations were available and were you involved in them?

The Civic Center and Men's Club. The Men's Club started in a barn.

What do you consider the biggest changes and when did they start changing?

With growth, you often have more challenges—we might see high-rises in the future.

Interview with Art Neubauer

How is Lindenhurst different now from 30, 40, 50 years ago?

I am a 48 year resident, and have held the role of village treasurer for over 40 years. The Plaza had a sign for a long time before it was actually built. There have been three additions to the original one. First American Bank was the first village bank. To catch the train you had to go to either Grayslake or Waukegan. Village offices were in a small building originally, which included four or five church pews that someone donated. After that, offices were in Plaza and then in 1968 the village built their own building—its current location.

Is there any particular person or event that you think is important in the village's history?

Thor Neumann—the civic center hall (Men's Club) was named after him—Thor did much for the village—also, Police Chief Ron Coles. He started to put the Lindenhurst Police Department together.

What has been the most radical change in the village since you have lived here?

I once knew everybody in town but now I only know a few—the village has experienced steady growth since its incorporation.

What has remained constant or the same since you have lived in the village?

The Linden Plaza—it has stayed largely the same since it was built.

What does Lindenhurst mean to you?

I liked Lindenhurst from the first minute I came here. It was a homey village with a good value for your money. When I first became treasurer, I would approve bills and then have to wait for funds to come in, but luckily, the village is no longer in the same straits. They have money in there to pay bills now.

978-0-595-50704-7
0-595-50704-2

Printed in the United States
114404LV00001B/205-744/P